W9-BHG-506

Love to Dance

Hip-Hop

Angela Royston

Heinemann
LIBRARY
Chicago, Illinois

www.capstonepub.com
Visit our website to find out more information about Heinemann-Raintree books.

To order:
☎ Phone 800-747-4992
🖥 Visit www.capstonepub.com
to browse our catalog and order online.

Edited by Nancy Dickmann, Catherine Veitch, and Abby Colich
Designed by Cynthia Della-Rovere
Picture research by Elizabeth Alexander
Production by Alison Parsons
Originated by Capstone Global Library Ltd
Printed in China.
112014 008625RP

Library of Congress Cataloging-in-Publication Data
Royston, Angela, 1945-
Hip-hop / Angela Royston.
   p. cm.—(Love to dance)
   Includes bibliographical references and index.
   ISBN 978-1-4109-4922-6 (hb)—ISBN 978-1-4109-4927-1 (pb) 1. Hip-hop dance. I. Title.
GV1796.H57R69 2013
793.3—dc23   2012019141

Acknowledgments

We would like to thank the following for permission to reproduce photographs: Alamy pp. 6, 18 (© AlamyCelebrity), 25 (© Lebrecht Music and Arts Photo Library); Corbis pp. 7 (© Erik Isakson), 13 (© Imaginechina), 17 (© Mango Productions), 22 (© Heide Benser), 23 (© Ted Soqui), 28 (© Anna Carnochan/Retna Ltd.), 29 (© Ocean); Getty Images pp. 8 (Jeff J Mitchell), 9 (Nick Onken/UpperCut Images), 15 (Phil Dent/Redferns), 16 (Ollie Millington/Redferns via Getty Images), 20 (Steven Lawton/FilmMagic), 21 (Dean Treml/Red Bull via Getty Images), 26 (Trae Patton/NBC/NBCU Photo Bank via Getty Images), 27 (Patrick Lin/AFP); Rex Features pp. 12 (Globe Photos Inc), 14 (Ray Tang); Shutterstock title page (© R. Gino Santa Maria), 4 (© chaoss), 5 (© R. Gino Santa Maria), 10 (© R. Gino Santa Maria), 11 (© Kovalev Sergey), 19 (© R. Gino Santa Maria); SuperStock p. 24 (© fstop).

Design features reproduced with permission of Shutterstock (© markrhiggins, © CAN BALCIOGLU, © Hannamariah, © Paul Clarke).

Cover photograph of a woman dancing hip-hop reproduced with permission of Getty Images (Larysa Dodz/Vetta).

We would like to thank Allen Desterhaft for his invaluable help in the preparation of this book.

Every effort has been made to contact copyright holders of material reproduced in this book. Any omissions will be rectified in subsequent printings if notice is given to the publisher.

All the Internet addresses (URLs) given in this book were valid at the time of going to press. However, due to the dynamic nature of the Internet, some addresses may have changed, or sites may have changed or ceased to exist since publication. While the author and publisher regret any inconvenience this may cause readers, no responsibility for any such changes can be accepted by either the author or the publisher.

Contents

This Is Hip-Hop!. 4

Breaking. 6

Dancing in the Street 8

Tricky Moves: Freezes. 10

Popping and Locking 12

Basic Move: Moonwalking 14

Dance Crews. .16

Hip-Hop Gear. 18

Competitions. .20

The Skills 22

Tricky Move: The Windmill 24

Where to See It 26

Give It a Try! 28

Glossary. *30*

Find Out More *31*

Index *32*

Some words are shown in bold, **like this**. You can find out what they mean by looking in the glossary.

This Is Hip-Hop!

Hip-hop is exciting. The dancers may start slowly, but soon their whole bodies are moving with the pounding music. They dip down, balance on one hand, and twist their legs in the air. The crowd cheers.

What's it all about?

Champion hip-hop dancer Roxrite says: "The best thing is that you feel free when you're doing it."

Breaking

Hip-hop dancing began in the 1970s. A **DJ** named DJ Kool Herc noticed that many kids waited for the musical break during a song before they danced. He looped, or repeated, the breaks to give them longer to dance.

DJ Kool Herc

B-boys and b-girls

DJ Kool Herc called the boys who took up **break dancing** b-boys, and he called the girls b-girls.

Dancing in the Street

Hip-hop began on the streets of New York City. B-boys showed off their moves on street corners and in school playgrounds, parks, and public spaces.

The battle

Hip-hop dancers take turns dancing.
They try to outdo each other's moves.
This is called a "**battle**."

Tricky Moves: Freezes

Freezes are for b-boys and b-girls with strong arms! In the baby freeze, dancers balance on their hands and head and bring their legs level with their waist. Then they freeze, or stay still—without falling over!

baby freeze

One-handed freeze

In the one-handed freeze, the dancer balances on just one hand.

11

Popping and Locking

There are many styles of hip-hop dancing. **Popping**, **locking**, and **boogaloo** are **funk** styles. They are less acrobatic than **break dancing**. The dancers make jerky moves, like robots, in time to the music.

popper Zhuo Jun

Electric Boogaloos

Boogaloo Sam invented popping and boogaloo. Sam called his group the "Electric Boogaloos".

Basic Move: Moonwalking

In moonwalking, dancers look as if they are moving forward when they are moving backward. To moonwalk, lift the heel of one foot and slide the other foot back. Then lift that heel and slide the first foot back.

Moonwalking is also called the backslide.

Famous moonwalker

Many dancers began moonwalking after they saw Michael Jackson doing it in his performances.

15

Dance Crews

Hip-hop is not just for dancing on your own. A **crew** is a group of dancers who create their own moves. Crews compete against each other in **battles**.

The dance crew Diversity became famous after winning a TV talent show in 2009.

Local friends

A crew is usually a group of friends from the same neighborhood. They dance together and experiment with new moves.

Hip-Hop Gear

Hip-hop dancers wear loose, comfortable clothes, such as baggy shirts and tracksuits. B-boys and b-girls like flashy jewelry, sneakers, and baseball caps.

Hip-hop culture

Hip-hop is closely linked to **rap**. Rap became popular when **DJs** began to speak over the musical breaks in songs.

Competitions

Hip-hop competitions are where **battles** count. There are different events for solo dancers and for **crews**. Some competitions are local and others are national.

Bubblegum Crew

Roxrite

The world's best dancers compete at Red Bull BC One and the World Hip-Hop Championships. These international competitions take place every year in different cities.

The Skills

To be a hip-hop dancer, you need a good ear for rhythm—your dance has to keep time to the music. You also have to be fit and able to move your body in lots of positions. Keep practicing your moves.

New styles

Hip-hop dancers keep creating new styles. Krumping, for example, is fast and involves jabs, arm swings, chest pops, and stomping.

23

Tricky Move: The Windmill

The windmill is a spectacular and difficult move. It starts with the baby **freeze** (see page 10), but then the dancer spins around with his or her legs slicing the air. It has to be seen to be believed!

This move is called the windmill, because the dancer's legs whirl like the sails of a windmill.

Where to See It

You can see hip-hop in music videos on television and on the Internet. Search online for videos of particular moves and performers. It is even more exciting to see hip-hop live, on the street, or in local competitions.

CJ Dippa on *America's Got Talent*

Worldwide

Hip-hop is popular in many countries, particularly in the United States, Japan, France, Britain, Australia, and South Korea.

Give It a Try!

Everyone can dance hip-hop! You do not have to be as good as the best dancers. Join a class or begin with a DVD and your friends. Get creative and give yourself a cool name.

The result?

You will have lots of fun and become fitter and healthier. Expressing yourself will make you feel more confident.

29

Glossary

battle contest between hip-hop dancers, in which each dancer or group tries to perform more impressive moves

boogaloo style of hip-hop dancing usually performed to funk music

break dancing fast, acrobatic dancing in which different parts of the body—especially the hands, arms, head, back, and hips—touch the ground

crew group of hip-hop dancers

DJ short for "disc jockey," a person who spins records and mixes music

freeze move in which a dancer freezes in a balance

funk style of music that was popular in the 1970s and 1980s

locking energetic style of dancing in which the dancer suddenly holds a position for a moment

popping funk and hip-hop style of dance in which the dancer clenches the muscles and then relaxes them so that the body jerks

rap style of music in which rhyming poetry is spoken over background music

Find Out More

Books

Cornish, Melanie J. *The History of Hip Hop*. New York: Crabtree, 2009.

Fitzgerald, Tamsin. *Hip-Hop and Urban Dance* (Dance). Chicago: Heinemann Library, 2009.

Freese, Joan. *Hip-Hop Dancing* (Snap Books). Mankato, Minn.: Capstone, 2008.

Websites

Facthound offers a safe, fun way to find Internet sites related to this book. All of the sites on Facthound have been researched by our staff.

Here's all you do:
Visit www.facthound.com

Type in this code: 9781410949226

Index

b-boys 7, 8, 10, 18
b-girls 7, 10, 18
baby freeze 10, 24
backslide 14
battles 9, 16, 20, 30
boogaloo 12, 13, 30
break dancing 7, 12, 30
Bubblegum Crew 20

CJ Dippa 26
classes 28
clothes 18
competitions 20–21, 26
confidence 29
crews 16–17, 20, 30

Diversity 16
DJ Kool Herc 6
DJs 6, 7, 19, 30

freezes 10–11, 24, 30
funk styles 12, 30

history of hip-hop 6–8

Jackson, Michael 15

krumping 23

locking 12, 30

moonwalking 14–15
music videos 26

one-handed freeze 11

popping 12, 13, 30

rap 19, 30
rhythm 22
Roxrite 5, 21

skills 22–23

windmill 24–25